Knock! Knock!

Who's there?

A Potty Training Picture Book

Written by
Nick Pierce

Illustrated by
Elissambura

SCRIBBLERS
a SALARIYA imprint

Who's there?

Sheep ALWAYS remembers to knock first before entering the bathroom.

Who's there?

Elephant
NEVER forgets to stay
near the potty after eating.

Who's there?

Giraffe!

Giraffe
Always uses the potty before she goes to sleep at night

...in case she gets the urge.

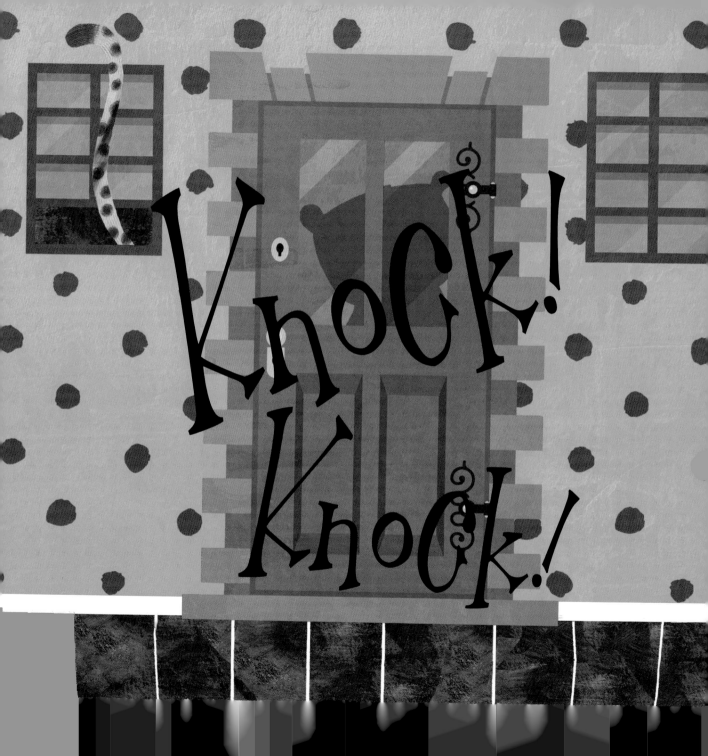

Who's there?

Cheetah ALWAYS leaves enough time to get to the toilet so he doesn't have to

Rrrrush!

KNOCK!
KNOCK!

litter tray

Who's there?

Cat

Tries not to fidget on the toilet in case

she makes a mess.

Who's there?

Hippo ALWAYS washes his hands after using the bathroom.

Who's there?

FOX ALWAYS closes the door when she's in the bathroom.

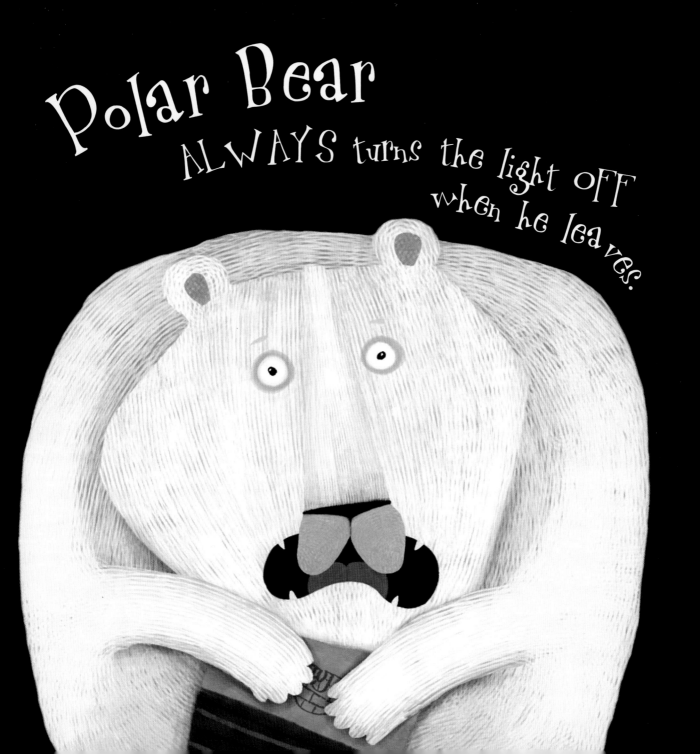

Who's there?

Horse ALWAYS wipes himself clean after he's finished.

Who's there?

Zebra
Reads or draws while on the potty to stop herself getting bored.

Who's there?

All of us!